Edward M Boykin

The Falling Flag

Evacuation of Richmond, Retreat and Surrender at Appomattox. Third

Edition

Edward M Boykin

The Falling Flag

Evacuation of Richmond, Retreat and Surrender at Appomattox. Third Edition

ISBN/EAN: 9783337081362

Printed in Europe, USA, Canada, Australia, Japan

Cover: Foto ©ninafisch / pixelio.de

More available books at **www.hansebooks.com**

A CAVALRY CHARGE.

THE FALLING FLAG.

EVACUATION OF RICHMOND,

RETREAT AND SURRENDER

AT

APPOMATTOX.

By EDWARD M. BOYKIN,

LT. COL. 7th REG'T S. C. CAVALRY.

Third Edition.

NEW YORK:
E. J. HALE & SON, PUBLISHERS,
MURRAY STREET.
1874.

Entered according to Act of Congress, in the year 1874, by
E. J. HALE & SON,
in the Office of the Librarian of Congress at Washington.

DEDICATION.

TO THE OFFICERS AND MEN OF THE

7th South Carolina Cavalry,

THIS

SHORT ACCOUNT OF AN INTERESTING PERIOD IN THEIR MILITARY HISTORY,

AND THAT OF

THE CAUSE THEY LOVED SO WELL, AND FOR WHICH THEY FOUGHT SO FAITHFULLY,

Is Dedicated,

BY ONE WHO CONSIDERS HAVING BEEN THEIR COMRADE THE PROUDEST RECOLLECTION OF HIS LIFE.

PREFACE.

THE writer only attempts to give some account of what occurred within his own observation; he would have esteemed it a privilege to enter into all the detail that lights up the last desperate struggle, made by that glorious remnant of the Army of Northern Virginia, with its skeleton battalions from every Southern State; illustrating their own fame and that of their noble leader, mile by mile, on that weary march from Richmond to Appomattox.

But he has confined himself to his own experiences, and in a great measure to what happened to his own Brigade, because it was written out, immediately after the war, from that standpoint. And if there be any merit in it, it is simply as a journal—what one man saw, and the impression produced thereby. This, even within a limited range, if truly put, represents at least a phase of the last act in the bloody drama that had been enacting for four years. More than this he could not hope to do, but leaves to abler hands the greater task that swells the current of events into the full tide of history.

CAMDEN, SOUTH CAROLINA,
June 15th, 1874.

EVACUATION OF RICHMOND, 1865.

On Saturday, the 1st day of April, 1865, orders reached us at camp headquarters of the Seventh South Carolina Cavalry, Gary's Brigade, to send forward all the dismounted men of the regiment to report to Lt. Col. Barham, Twenty-fourth Regiment Virginia Cavalry, in command of dismounted men of the brigade, for duty on the lines. Began to think that a move was intended of some sort, but on the brink, as all knew and felt for some time, of great events, it was difficult to say what was expected. On Sunday, the 2d, about mid-day, orders came for the wagon train of the brigade, spare horses, baggage of all sorts, that was to go at all—the greater part was to be left—to move into Richmond at once, and fall into the general train of the army of the north bank of the James River. Richmond then was to be evacuated, so all felt, though no public statement of the fact had been made; heavy fighting had been going on during the day, in the neighborhood of Petersburg, but there had been one unceasing roar of battle around us for months, and no particular account was taken of that.

The brigade was ordered to move after nightfall from its position (our winter quarters) between the

Williamsburg and the "Nine Mile" road, about four miles from Richmond, and immediately behind the outer line of works on the edge of the battle field of the "Seven Pines."

We moved after dark—the Seventh South Carolina, Col. Haskell; the Hampton Legion, South Carolina, Lieut. Col. Arnold; the Twenty-fourth Virginia, Col. Robbins, and a small party of the Seventh Georgia, part of a company only—Gen. Gary commanding the brigade.

The Seventh Georgia were, with the exception spoken of, dismounted, though belonging to our brigade. We halted on the Charles City road, found all the infantry gone; Gen. Longstreet, who commanded on the north bank, had been withdrawn with Gen. Field's Division across the river, to reinforce Gen. Lee around Petersburg, some two or three days before, leaving only the Division of Gen. Kershaw in our immediate neighborhood, and Gen. Custis Lee in command of the Marine Brigade and City Reserves, next the river, near Fort Gilmer, all under the command of Lt. Gen. Ewell; also Hankin's Battery, Virginia, attached to our brigade.

We were to wait until two o'clock, and as soon as our dismounted men, who were filling the place of infantry pickets withdrawn, should come in, we were to move on to the city, acting as "rear guard," and burn Mayo's Bridge. It was all out now; there had been a heavy fight in the morning, near Petersburg, Gen. Lee all but overwhelmed, Gen. A. P. Hill killed, and the army in full retreat on Burkville, to effect, if possible, a junction with Gen. Johnston, in North Carolina.

We built big fires of brush wood, to give light and warmth, and deceive the enemy. It was cold, though in April; the men, as usual, light-hearted and cheerful round the fires, though an empire was passing away around them; some, with an innate consciousness of the work before them, when they heard that the halt was to be for two or three hours, wrapped in their overcoats, with the capes drawn over their heads, were soon sound asleep, forgetting the defeat of armies, the work of yesterday, the toil and danger of to-morrow, in some quiet dream of a home perhaps never seen again.

Two o'clock came and passed; our men had not come in. The General waited until four o'clock. I think we were at this point six miles from Richmond. We should have been there at daylight, and we were to burn the bridge in time to prevent the enemy's crossing, as our whole train, with infantry and artillery, had crossed during the night. Our brigade of cavalry, and one company of artillery attached to it, were all that were on this side—the north bank of the river. We could wait no longer, and moved off slowly. In a short time after we started a tremendous explosion took place toward the river, lighting up everything like day, and waking every echo, and every Yankee for thirty miles around. It was evidently a gunboat on the river at "Drury's

Bluff." Two others followed, but they did not equal the first. She was iron-clad—the "Virginia," as we afterwards heard—just completed. She burst like a bomb-shell, and told, in anything but a whisper, the desperate condition of things. There was no time to be lost; the Yankees had heard it as well as ourselves, and we moved on at once.

We overtook, just at daylight, and passed a small squad of our dismounted men from the Seventh, who had got in from the picket line. When we reached the intermediate line of works, where the "Charles City" and "New Kent" roads come together, not far from the "turnpike gate," which all who travelled that road—and who of the army of Northern Virginia did not?—will remember, the sun was just rising, and an ugly red glare showed itself in the direction of Richmond that dimmed the early sunshine.

At this point the General determined (though expecting the enemy's cavalry every moment) to occupy the works, and wait for the dismounted men. The guns of the battery that accompanied us were placed in position, and our men dismounted and occupied the lines on the right and left of the road. In about a half hour's time, and to our great satisfaction—for it seemed a hard case to leave the poor tired fellows to be gobbled up—a straggling line of tired men and poor walkers, as dismounted cavalry always must be in their big boots and spurs, showed themselves over the hill, dragged themselves along, and passed on before us into the city. We followed on, went down the steep hill by the house where General Johnston's headquarters were about the time of the retreat from Yorktown, and got into the river road, and so had the enemy behind us. It was here he might have cut us off from the city and secured the bridge.

We passed into the "Rockets," the southern suburb of Richmond, at an easy marching gait, and there learned that the bridge had taken fire from some of the buildings, which by this time we could see were on fire in the city. Fearing our retreat would be cut off at that point, which would throw us from our position as rear-guard, we pushed on rapidly, the column moving at a trot through the "Rockets."

The peculiar population of that suburb were gathered on the sidewalk; bold, dirty looking women, who had evidently not been improved by four years' military association, dirtier (if possible) looking children, and here and there skulking, scoundrelly looking men, who in the general ruin were sneaking from the holes they had been hiding in—not, though, in the numbers that might have been expected, for the great crowd, as we soon saw, were hard at it, pillaging the burning city. One strapping virago stood on the edge of the pavement with her arms akimbo, looking at us with intense scorn as we swept along; I could have touched her with the toe of my boot as I rode by her, closing the rear of the column; she caught my eye—"Yes," said she, with all of Tipperary in her brogue, "afther fighting them for four years ye're running like dawgs!" The woman was either drunk or very much in earnest, for I give her credit for feeling all she said, and her son or husband had to do his own fighting, I will answer for it, wherever he was, or get no kiss or comfort from her. But I could not stop to explain that General Longstreet's particular orders were not to make a fight in the city, if it could be avoided, so I left her to the enjoyment of her own notions, unfavorable as they evidently were to us.

On we went across the creek, leaving a picket at that point to keep a lookout for the enemy, that we knew must now be near upon our heels. It was after seven o'clock, the sun having been up for some time. After getting into Main street and passing the two tobacco warehouses opposite one another, occupied as prisons in the early years of the war, we met the motley crowd thronging the pavement, loaded with every species of plunder.

Bare-headed women, their arms filled with every description of goods, plundered from warehouses and shops, their hair hanging about their ears, were rushing one way to deposit their plunder and return for more, while a current of the empty-handed surged in a contrary direction towards the scene.

The roaring and crackling of the burning houses, the trampling and snorting of our horses over the paved streets as we swept along, wild sounds of every description, while the rising sun came dimly through the cloud of smoke that hung like a pall around him, made up a scene that beggars description, and which I hope never to see again—the saddest of many of the sad sights of war—a city undergoing pillage at the hands of its own mob, while the standards of an empire were being taken from its capitol, and the tramp of a victorious enemy could be heard at its gates.

Richmond had collected within its walls the refuse of the war—thieves and deserters, male and female, the vilest of the vile were there, but strict military discipline had kept it down. Now, in one moment, it was all removed—all restraint was taken off—and you may imagine the consequences. There were said to be 5,000 deserters in the city, and you could see the grey jackets here and there sprinkled in the mob that was roaring down the street. When we reached somewhere between Twentieth and Twenty-fifth streets—I will not be certain—the flames swept across Main street so we could not pass. The column turned to the right, and so got into the street above it. On this (Franklin street) are many private residences; at the windows we could see the sad and tearful faces of the kind Virginia women, who had never failed the soldier in four long years of war and trouble, ready to the last to give him devoted attendance in his wounds and sickness, and to share with his necessities the last morsel.

These are strong but not exaggerated expressions. Thousands, yes, tens of thousands, from the Rio Grande to the Potomac, can bear witness to the truth of everything I say. And it was a sad thought to every man that was there that day, that we seemed, as a compensation for all that they had done for us, to be leaving them to the mercy of the enemy; but their own General Lee was gone before, and we were but as the last wave of the receding tide.

After getting round the burning square we turned back towards the river. The portion of Mayo's, or rather the lesser bridge that crossed the canal, had taken fire from the large flouring mill near it, and was burning, but not the main bridge; so we followed the cross street below the main approach to the bridge, at the foot of which was a bridge across the canal, forcing our horses through the crowd of pillagers gathered at this point, greater than at any other—they had broken into some government stores. A low white man—he seemed a foreigner—was about to strike a woman over a barrel of flour under my horse's nose, when a stout negro took her part and threatened to throw him into the canal. We were the rear regiment at this time. All this occurred at one of those momentary halts to which the rear of a marching column is subjected; in another moment we moved on, the crowd closed in, and we saw no more. After crossing the canal we were obliged to go over a stone conduit single file.

At last we were on the main bridge, along which were scattered faggots to facilitate the burning. Lieut. Cantey, Sergt. Lee and twenty men from the Seventh were left, under the supervision of Colonel Haskell, to burn the bridge, while the rest went slowly up the hill on which Manchester is built, and waited for them. Just as the canal bridge on which we had crossed took fire, about forty of Kautz' cavalry galloped easily up Main street, fired a long shot with their carbines on the party at the bridge, but went on up the street instead of coming down to the river. They were too late to secure the bridge, if that had been their object, which they seemed to be aware of, as they made no attempt to do so. Their coming was of service to the city. General Ord, as we afterwards understood, acted with promptness and kindness, put down the mob, and put out the fire, and protected the people of Richmond from the mob and his own soldiers, in their persons and property.

As we sat upon our horses on the high hill on which Manchester is built, we looked down upon the City of Richmond. By this time the fire appeared to be general. Some magazine or depot for the manufacture of ordnance stores was on fire about the centre of the city; it was marked by the peculiar blackness of smoke; from the middle of it would come the roar of bursting shells and boxes of fixed ammunition, with flashes that gave it the appearance of a thunder cloud of huge proportions with lightning playing through it. On our right was the navy yard, at which were several steamers and gunboats on fire, and burning in the river, from which the cannon were thundering as the fire reached them. The old war-scarred city seemed to prefer annihilation to conquest—a useless sacrifice, as it afterwards proved, however much it may have added to the grandeur of the closing scene; but such is war.

Moving slowly out of Manchester, we soon got among the host of stragglers, who, from a natural fear of the occupation of the towns both of Petersburg and Richmond, were going with the rear of our army. Civilians, in some cases ladies of gentle nurture, without means of conveyance, were sitting on their trunks by the roadside—refugees from Petersburg to Richmond a few days before, now refugees from Richmond into the highway; indeed the most were from Petersburg, driven out literally by the artillery fire. The residents of Richmond, as a general thing, remained.

Two ladies here got into our regimental ambulance, rode for a few miles, and then took refuge in some farm house, I suppose, as they disappeared before the day was over.

By the roadside, or rather the sidewalk, were sitting on their bags some hardy, weather-beaten looking men. They were what was left of the crew of the "famous Alabama," and had just landed from the gunboats that had been blown up on the river, which had first started us on our march. Admiral Semmes was with them; I remember some of our young men jesting with the bronzed veterans, but we did not then know the renowned Captain of the great Confederate war ship was there in person, or he certainly should not have had to complain of being left standing in the road and dusted by the "young rascals of the cavalry rear-guard," as he does in his book. Some one of the "young cavalry rascals" would have been dismounted, and his horse given to the man who had carried our flag so far and fought it so well.

Acting as rear-guard, we moved very slowly, giving time for all stragglers, wagons and worn out artillery horses to close up. Already we began to come upon a piece of artillery mired down, the horses dead beat, the gun left, and the horses double-teamed into the remaining pieces. So we went into camp that night, after marching all day, only eleven miles from Richmond, on the "Burkville road." Burkville is the point at which the railroad branches west to Lynchburg and south to Danville, and was our objective point.

The brigade went into camp, or bivouac rather, by squadrons, in a piece of woods, the men picketing their horses immediately behind their camp fires. The fires burned brightly, the horses ate the corn the men had brought in their bags and what forage they could get hold of during the day. Our surgeon, Dr. McLaurin, had gotten up his ambulance, and helped out our bread and bacon with a cup of coffee and some not very salt James River herring, that he had among his stores—and so ended the first day's march.

We did not move until nearly nine o'clock next morning, as at our slowest marching gait we out-travelled the march we were covering. The day was spent in following after the movements of the army. Occasional pieces of artillery left upon the roadside showed that the horses were giving out. After dark we crossed the Appomattox, some twenty or twenty-five miles from Richmond, at the railroad bridge, which was planked over so our horses could cross. After crossing the river we went into camp about a mile beyond, surrounded by most of the infantry of the north bank, General Longstreet's immediate command, the men leading their horses over. One of the young men attached to our mess, a good looking young fellow, had his pockets filled with ham and biscuits near the crossing by some good Samaritan he had met, and so our herring, grilled by one of the couriers on the half of a canteen, was helped out by this addition.

We were suddenly roused in the night by a fire in the dry grass on which we were sleeping. It caught from our camp fire and was among our blankets before we knew it. There was a general jumping up and stamping it out. One of the men created quite a sensation by shaking his India rubber, which was on fire; it flew to pieces in a shower of flame. The effect of the night attack is still shown in the blistered and scorched condition of my field-glasses. We were at this point but a few miles from Amelia Court House, between which and our camp of that night the road from Petersburg joins the road from Richmond, and the two columns respectively met—the two streams flowed into one—forming what was left of Lee's great army of Northern Virginia—the men exchanging in the fresh morning air kindly greetings with one another, from Texas to Maryland, from the Potomac to the Rio Grande. They marched along, leaving their fate in the hands of the great leader they knew so well and had trusted so long.

About a mile or two from Amelia Court House our brigade was ordered to graze their horses in a clover field, still keeping the regiments together as near as could be in squadrons, for we could make no calculations, as will be seen, upon the movements of the enemy's cavalry. Colonel Haskell, Colonel Robbins, of the Twenty-fourth Virginia, and myself were seated upon the steps of an old house, breakfasting with Colonel Robbins, who had been fortunate enough to meet a friend who had filled his haversack, and shared his good luck with us, watching the men and horses who were eating what they could get, when here it came at last: "Mount the brigade and move up at once!" The enemy had gotten in force between us and Burkville, and his cavalry had struck our wagon and ordnance train some three or four miles from where we were. So there was mounting in hot haste, and off we went at a gallop.

We soon reached the point they had first attacked and set fire to the wagons—the canvas covers taking fire very easily. Their plan of operation seemed to be to strike the train, which was several miles long at a given point, fire as many wagons as their number admitted of doing at once, then making a circuit and striking it again, leaving an intermediate point untouched.

We did not suppose the troops actually engaged in the firing exceeded three or four hundred well mounted men, but had a large body of cavalry moving parallel with them in easy supporting distance. This was a very effectual mode of throwing the march of the wagon train into confusion, independent of the absolute destruction they caused.

The burning caissons, as we rode by, were anything but pleasant neighbors, and were exploding right and left, but I do not recollect of any of our men being hit by them.

We could hear the enemy ahead of us, as we pressed our tired horses through the burning wagons and the scattered plunder which filled the road, giving our own wagon-rats and skulkers a fine harvest of plunder. Many of the wagons were untouched, but standing in the road without horses, the teamsters at the first alarm taking them out and making for the woods, coming back and taking their wagons again after the stampede was over, sometimes to find them plundered by our own cowardly skulkers, that I suppose belong to all armies. I have no doubt Cæsar had them in his tenth legion, and Xenophon in his famous ten thousand.

So far the enemy, in carrying out his plan of attack, had kept in motion; but after passing a large creek that crosses the road and runs on by "Amelia Springs," they halted at an old field on the side of the road and made a front. As the head of our column crossed the creek a lady was standing in the mud by the road side with a soldier in a "grey jacket." She had been with the ordnance train—the ambulance in which she had been riding was taken, the horses carried off, and as we closed up she was left as we found her. She was from Mississippi, and had left Richmond with her friends in the "Artillery," and was much more mad than scared, and she stood there in the mud (she was young and pretty) and gesticulated as she told her story, making up a picture striking and peculiar. There was no time to listen, but promising to do our best to punish the aggressors, who had taken her up and dropped her so unceremoniously in the mud, which was the amount of the damage, and advising her to take shelter in a large white house on the hill, we moved on to meet the party ahead, who, near enough their reserve now for support, had halted to give us a taste of their quality.

At first they called out to come on and get their "greenbacks," seeing the small party in advance with the General, but as the regiments rode into the field, which was large enough to make a display of the entire line, they stood but to exchange a scattering fire, and then moved in retreat along a road running parallel to the main road and leading to "Amelia Springs." The Seventh, from position, was the leading regiment, and moved at a gallop in pursuit. The road swept round a point of wood on the left and an old field on the right grown up with pine. In advance rode five well mounted men of the regiment, as a lookout, led by the adjutant—General Gary immediately behind them—and the head of our column, the Seventh cavalry, next. As the advance guard rounded the bend in the road it was swept by the fire of the enemy, who had halted for that purpose, wheeling instantly in retreat as soon as they delivered their fire. Four men out of the five, all except the adjutant, were hit, one of them in the spine, "Mills," an approved scout, and one of the best and bravest men in the army. Throwing his arms over his head with a yell of agony, wrung from him by intense pain, he pitched backwards off his horse, which was going at full speed. The horse, a thoroughbred mare, kept on with us in the rush. (I will here say that I never saw the young man again—he was just in front of me when he fell—until three or four years after, in a pulpit, as a Presbyterian preacher. He had gotten over his wound without its doing him permanent injury). On we went, picking up some of the rear of the party who had not moved quick enough. The main body had gotten where there were thick woods on both sides of the road, where they halted to make a stand. But we were upon them before they made their wheel to face to the rear, or rather while they were in the act of making it, and so had them at advantage; we were among them with the sabre. The work was short and sharp, and we drove them along the road clear of the wood into the open field, where there was a strong dismounted reserve. Here we caught a fire that dropped two of our leading horses —Captain Caldwell's and Lieutenant Hinson's. Caldwell's horse was killed dead. Hinson's fell with a broken leg, catching his rider under him and holding him until relieved. A heavy fire swept the woods and road, so we dismounted the brigade as fast as the men came up, extending the dismounted line along the front of the enemy's fire, and moving to the left as he fell back to a stronger position. As we moved in advance they gave up the position by the house they had first taken, fell back across the field and ravine to the top of the opposite hill, where they halted in force and threw up temporary breastworks, made from a rail fence, and from that position repeated the invitation to "Come and get greenbacks." We moved up, occupied the ravine immediately in their front, which was deep enough to shelter the mounted officers, the line officers and the men being dismounted. Here General Gary determined to hold his position, until General Fitz Lee, who commanded our cavalry, came up, not deeming it advisable to attack the enemy in his present position and numbers. In half an hour's time General Fitz Lee came up with his division, dismounted his men, formed line, flanked the position, charged it in front, two or three heavy volleys, a shout and a rush. The enemy finding his position untenable moved off to the main body, not more than two or three miles from them—moving rapidly, as we found several of their wounded on the roadside, left in the hurry of their retreat. We moved on slowly after them—the sun being nearly down—to "Amelia Springs," some two miles off, crossed the creek, and, though we had commenced the fight in the morning, were politely requested (everybody knows what a military request is) by General Lee to move down the road until we could see the Yankee pickets, put the brigade into camp, post pickets, and make the best of it—all of which we did.

We did not have far to go to find the pickets—about a mile; posted our own two or three hundred yards from the brigade; sent to the mill on the creek at "Amelia Springs" and drew rations of flour and bacon.

I had here one of those unexpected surprises that sometimes gleam upon us under the most unpropitious circumstances. As we rode up to the big white house on the hill General Fitz Lee stood giving orders for the disposition of the troops. Our men were in numbers filling their canteens with water at the well in the yard, when a lieutenant from the Hampton Legion came from the well with his canteen in his hand. "B.," I said, "I am very thirsty; will you give me a drink from your canteen?" "Certainly, sir," said he, and handed it to me. I took a large swallow and discovered it was excellent old apple brandy. I had eaten nothing since a very light breakfast; had been working hard in the saddle all day; had the breath knocked out of my body by a spent ball on the chest at the close of the charge in the woods; the excitement of the fight was over, and I was lying over the pommel, rather than sitting on my saddle, but as that electric fluid went down my throat I straightened up like a soldier at the word of command; I felt a new life pouring through my veins, and the worry and care of the situation was all gone, and I was ready for what was to come next— such is the power of contrast. B., who was watching me, raised a warning finger not to betray his secret, for what was a canteen of apple brandy to that crowd, that would not be denied? so I concealed my satisfaction and his secret, but have never forgotten my obligation to Lieutenant B. of the Hampton Legion.

All around us through the stillness floated the music of the Yankee bands, mocking with their beautiful music our desperate condition; yet our men around their fires were enjoying it as much, and, seemingly, with as light hearts as the owners of it. Occasionally, as a bugle call would ring out, which always sounds to a trooper as a challenge to arms, a different expression would show itself, and a harder look take the place of the softer one induced by "Home, Sweet Home," or "Annie Lawrie."

. So we made our bivouac in sight of the enemy's pickets, eating our homely rations with the keen relish and appetite health and hard work give. While our neighbors, whose interest in us could not be questioned, gave us the benefit of many a soft air, that told of other and very different scenes, we, in the language of romance, addressed ourselves to slumber, expecting an attack at or before daylight. This was our first night in sight of their outposts, and we had yet to learn their plan of attack. The game was in the toils and they meant to play a sure hand, with no more waste of material than was absolutely necessary. There was no night attack that I recollect in the course of the retreat. General Grant's large force seemed to be kept perfectly in hand, massed with great care to strike with effect at any given point on our line of march, gain the result of an overwhelming attack in force, and draw off in time to prevent disorder among their own troops—a wise arrangement under the circumstances.

Another pleasing incident occurred at this camp, as everything is relative and is great or little, according to circumstances. One of the non-commissioned officers of my old company came to me and asked if I would like to have my canteen filled with some very fine old apple brandy. One of General Lee's couriers had found a barrel of it covered up with leaves in an adjoining piece of woods, and let a few of his friends into the secret. Would I? Of course I would, and if we ever came out ahead I would recommend him for promotion. The canteen came full, and proved to be of the same tap as the " long swallow " was of which I had partaken so unexpectedly. That canteen of apple brandy, like Boniface's ale, was meat and drink for the rest of the time I was a soldier of the Southern Confederacy.

We got off about eight o'clock in the morning, not having been disturbed, as we expected, moved back across the creek that runs through the meadows at the foot of the hill below the hotel at " Amelia

Springs," halted and formed line, facing to the rear along the creek, from the ford at the road down the creek to the mill, destroyed the bridge, and held the position as rear-guard, until General Lee, whose camp was above us on the hill, around the hotel, formed his column and moved, we following slowly in the rear.

We marched that day, until the afternoon, among the infantry, artillery and wagons, going towards Farmville, on the Appomattox river and the Lynchburg railroad. There was a bridge across the river, at which, as was afterwards shown, it was General Lee's purpose to cross his infantry wagons and artillery.

We had been having a very tiresome march on our worn-out horses, through the fields on the side of the road, giving up the road proper to the wagon trains and troops, sometimes dismounting and leading our horses, to relieve them as much as possible.

About two or three o'clock we saw the infantry in front of us breaking from the line of march by brigades into a large field on the left of the road, and rapidly forming into compact masses in proper position and relation with one another, to be used as might be required. We halted and did the same, being the only cavalry at that point. We soon heard heavy firing on another road over to the right, two or three miles from us, artillery and small arms, and nearer to us—not a mile—was a lesser fight going on, to which we moved at once. The last, which was over before we got to it, was between General Lee's division of cavalry and a body of the enemy's infantry. They were, as we were told, a fresh set of troops who had just come on, and were literally gobbled up by Lee. We met the prisoners —some eight or nine hundred—going to the rear. Their coats were so new and blue, and buttons so bright, and shirts so clean, that it was a wonder to look upon them by our rusty lot.

They were pushing on to coöperate with the larger movement that was going on to the right, and fell in with General Lee's cavalry, and after a very respectable fight had their military experience brought to an abrupt conclusion. Lee's men had possessed themselves of a complete set of new brass instruments that formed their band.

The fight on the right was the heaviest and most damaging to us that occurred on the retreat, and is known as the Battle of "Sailor's Creek," or "High Bridge," where the divisions of General Kershaw and General Custis Lee, under the command of Lieutenant General Ewell, were knocked to pieces—and General Richard Anderson's command, composed of Pickett's Division and Bushrod Johnson's, with Huger's artillery. Pickett's and Huger's commands were, I think, destroyed, but Johnson managed to get through. Generals Kershaw, Ewell and Lee were, I know, taken prisoners. All this we knew nothing of at the time, only that there was heavy fighting, and that being a matter of course, excited no surprise.

The sun was nearly down and we moved towards Farmville, to go into camp for the night. It was after dark when we got there, went through the town to the grove on the other side, and made the best of it. We lived upon what we could pick up, as we had no wagons with us, and our servants and spare horses were with the wagon train.

The most fruitful source of supply was when we passed a broken down commissary wagon. The men would fill their haversacks with whatever they could find; and whatever they got, either in this way or at the country houses, was liberally shared with their friends and officers.

By a big fire we lay down, and slept the sleep of the tired. The nights were cold, so near the mountains, and, with light coverings on the cold ground, the burning down of the fire was a general awakening and building up of the same. At one of these movements we were surprised to find, between Colonel H. and myself, two men, who, attracted by the fire, cold and tired, had crept to its friendly warmth, making a needless apology for their presence. We found one to be a colonel of Pickett's division, the other a lieutenant, and realized fully how complete the destruction of that famous fighting division must have been as an organization, that we should find a regimental commander who did not know where to look for its standard. There seemed to be no particular hurry in getting off in the morning. We were waiting for orders by our fire, and filled up the time pressing horses in the town, from a kind consideration of the feelings of the owners, that they should not fall into the hands of the Yankees, much to the disgust of the said owners, who seemed much to prefer (good men and true as they were) the possible chance of the Yankee to the certainty of the Confederate abstraction.

One or two amusing incidents occurred in that connection. One of our young lieutenants had heard of a very fine bay stallion, belonging to a gentleman in town, and as the rumor had spread that pressing horse flesh was going on, he went off promptly with a man or two, reached the house, and was met at the door by a young and pretty woman, who, with all the elegant kindness of a Virginia lady, asked him to come in. He felt doubtful, but could not resist; ordering his men to hold on a minute or two, while he talked horse with the lady, wishing, in the innocent kindness of his heart, to break it to her gently. After a few minutes' general conversation he touched on the horse question. "Oh! yes, sir," she said, getting up and looking through a window that overlooked the back yard. "Yes, sir; I am sorry to disappoint you, but as you came in at the front door my husband was saddling the bay, and while you were talking to me I saw him riding out of the back gate. I am so sorry; *indeed I am.*" With a hasty good morning our lieutenant rode back to camp upon a horse some degrees below the standard of a "Red Eye" or any other race horse. The laugh was with the lady.

Another case was against a class who met with but little sympathy from a soldier in the field—a local or collecting quartermaster, *when of a particular class*—some able bodied young man, every way fit for the soldier, except in spirit, getting the position to screen himself from field duty and make money out of a suffering people. The order had been given through the brigade to take the horses wherever they could be found. A wagon with two good horses drove between our fire and that of the squadron lying next. A captain stepped out, stopped the wagon, and the horses were taken out and appropriated—the boy driving them ran off—and soon there came riding up a dashing young quartermaster on a fine grey horse, groomed to perfection, and horse and rider redolent of the sybaritism of the department, claimed the horses as belonging to *his department*, with a most insolent air, looking daggers and court martials, and swelling as only overfed subsistence agents on home duty could do. While he was talking I saw Captain D. walking round him looking at the gallant grey, and then at our colonel inquiringly. A nod from the colonel and Captain D's hand was on the grey's bridle, and a quiet but firm request, that sounded very much like an order, for him to get down, as his horse was wanted for cavalry service. The man of the subsistence and transportation department was so dumbfounded that he would have let pass the best operation possible of making money out of the necessities of the people for which his tribe was famous; but just then a bugle rang out the call for "boot and saddle;" the bugles of the other regiments took it up; the momentary diversion of the horse pressing and the quartermaster was forgotten; work was at hand; the rumbling of the artillery and wagons crossing the bridge, with columns of infantry between, could be heard down in the town at the foot of the hill, and the cavalry were wanted on the other side of the town, by the Randolph House, to hold the enemy in check and cover the crossing of the river.

The brigade was soon in the saddle, and moving at a swinging trot down the long street that constitutes mainly the town of Farmville. As the regiment passed a large building on the right, which was shown to be a boarding school for young ladies, from the number gathered on the piazza in front, we were greeted by their waving handkerchiefs and moist eyes, while cheer after cheer rose from our men in response to their kindness and sympathy. They did not know, as we did, that their friends and defenders were to pass by, leaving them so soon in the hands most dreaded by them. They saw us going to the front; our men were excited by the circumstances and the prospect of a fight, and the light of that wild glory that belongs to war shone over it all. The rough, grey soldier, the tramping column, and the groups of tender girls, mixed with it like flowers on a battle field, incongruous in detail, but blending with the picture, like discords in music, making it complete.

So on through the town, across the little stream,

and up the hill, on the top of which on the right stood a large white building, called, as I recollect, the Randolph House; in the field around were gathered and gathering large bodies of our cavalry, under the command of General F. H. Lee, General Rosser and other distinguished cavalry officers. We took our position among them. As before stated, our column, artillery and wagon train, were pouring in a steady stream across the bridge, and the enemy were pressing up their artillery, and already throwing long shots at it from batteries not near enough to do much if any harm, and too much under cover to admit of an effectual attack from us.

General Lee dismounted the most of his command and formed a line of battle along the road looking toward the point from which the enemy were advancing.

We (our brigade) were kept in the saddle at the point we first occupied on the right of the road. There was a house some three hundred yards from the road on the left, directly in front of General Lee's line, in a grove of oak, with a lane or avenue leading to it from the main road. Behind the house a battery seemed gradually advancing and already throwing its shells at or about the bridge. So far they were completely masked by the house, and we could only judge of their movements from their fire, which seemed closer every moment.

In pursuance of some order we changed our position, and rode to General Lee's dismounted line of battle. As we rode up—our regiment, the Seventh, leading—we were the right flank regiment in the brigade formation, and in column with the right in front were necessarily in advance. The battery seemed by this time to have gotten immediately behind the house, and was pitching shells about the bridge and into the town (the bridge was at the foot of the street) with precision and rapidity. Expecting to see it unmask itself in front of the house every moment, General Lee said to our colonel, "Haskell, as soon as that battery shows itself take it with your regiment; you can do it."

We moved at once down the avenue toward the house up to the edge of the oak wood, with which the lawn in front was surrounded, formed the regiment in column of fours in the road. The colonel rode along the side of the column, the adjutant detailing three of the best mounted men from each company—the horses were the animals specially selected—the *men* at that stage of the game were all known to be good—making thirty men, and the senior captain, Doby, in immediate command of the party.

The colonel rode in front of the halted column some forty or fifty yards, with his thirty men, after directing the officer next in command to ride down the flank of the regiment, form, and speak to each "set of fours" separately. Each set of fours waited for the word of command to be given to themselves specially, and as the order was given "to close up and dress," they did so steadily and firmly, and I looked into the eyes of each man in the regiment, and they looked into mine. There was little left for words to say.

There we sat, waiting to charge the battery that was momentarily expected to unmask in front of the house—something over two hundred men of the thousand on our muster roll, and all the cavalry of the army of Northern Virginia, looking on to see how we did it.

The shells from the battery whistled four or five feet above our heads, for they had discovered our line on the hill and turned their fire on it. The shells went over our heads, but struck a few feet in front of General Lee's dismounted line, making gaps in it as they did so.

Just then information was received that our marching column had crossed the bridge—our charge was not to be—there was nothing to wait for. General Lee mounted his men, formed, and moved off promptly to cross the river at a ford some two miles farther up, leaving General Gary with his brigade to cover his retreat. We drew off from the position we had taken to attack the battery, the regiment resuming its position at the head of the brigade, with the exception of Colonel Haskell, Captain Doby, and the thirty men before chosen—this party remained in the rear of the brigade, all moving off slowly, the last of General Lee's division having by this time gone out of sight over the top of the hill.

We had not yet been able to perceive that the bridge was on fire. General Gary said that General

Lee had left it to his discretion to cross at the bridge if he could, as he expected we would be pressed very closely at the last; so, instead of following General Lee's line of retreat, we turned down towards the town again and halted in the street while the General himself galloped down to the bridge to see if it was practicable. The shells were bursting over the town, and in the street occasionally, while the good people of Farmville, in a state of great though natural alarm, were leaving with their goods forthwith. We told them we were going at once; were not to make a fight in the town; to keep quiet in their. houses, and it was not probable they would be interfered with.

The bridge, bursting into smoke and flame, told the story before the General got back. On we went up the street, through the grove where we camped the night before, on toward the railroad, following the track taken by General Lee.

Just beyond the wood, on the outskirts of the town, a large creek runs under the railroad through an arched way or viaduct, wide enough for the road to pass along its bank. After crossing this creek, on a bridge on the town side of the railroad embankment, we passed along the road under the culvert, and formed on the edge of the woods some three or four hundred yards beyond. Colonel Haskell, with Captain Doby and his thirty men, halted at the bridge to destroy it, as by this time bodies of the enemy's cavalry could be seen moving at a gallop on the hill above. The creek was too deep for a ford; so it was all important, in connection with our crossing the river, to check their advance by burning the bridge. Colonel Haskell, dismounting, placed all of his party, except his axemen, behind the railroad bank which overlooked the bridge and served as a capital breastwork, went to work with a will. By this time the enemy was upon them and commenced a heavy fire, which was returned handsomely by the party under cover and with good effect. Colonel Haskell succeeded in the complete destruction of the bridge, with the loss of only one of his axemen killed.

The cover of the bank, and the small number actually exposed when at work, enabled him to perform a gallant and dangerous piece of service with slight loss.

General Gary, who had occupied a position between the wood where the brigade was formed and near where the bridge party was at work, so as to be in complete command of whatever might take place, moved on at once toward the ford where General Lee had already crossed his division. We moved by regiments in intervals after him.

By some mistake of our guide we were carried to a point in the river which was not practicable, at the then stage of the river, as a ford—which we duly discovered after nearly drowning two or three men and horses of the ambulance train, whom we found at the head of the column when we reached the river, their usual place being in the rear. The adjutant, finding them in front, asked them, "What the deuce are you doing here—your place is in the rear?" "No, sir," said a long-backed individual of the party, in a copper colored raiment, who seemed to have been making a study of the rules and regulations as applying to his own department. "Not so. In the rear, I grant you, in the advance; in the front, if you please, in a retreat." "So be it," said I. "In with you;" and in they went, nothing loth. The river was swimming and the horses swam badly, making plunges to reach the opposite bank, which, when they gained, was steep and treacherous, and it was only after repeated efforts, and their riders getting off into the river, that they made a landing. It was apparent that this could not be the point that General Lee had crossed his division. Some one turned up who led us right. About a mile farther up we found the ford that he had crossed at, and got over without difficulty or molestation; it was scarcely swimming to the smallest horse, and directly opposite lay all of the Virginia cavalry to cover our crossing, if pressed, while it was going on. We were the first regiment that crossed; found some stacks of oats; halted, formed in squadrons, fed our horses, ate what we had to eat, rested, and, as usual, made the best of it.

After a rest of about an hour General Lee moved off, we following in his rear, the Virginians ahead of us with General Lee destroying the equanimity of the good people on their line of march by pressing every horse found in their way. It seemed hard to come down so on our own people, after all the sacrifices already made by them, but if the horse was lost by our taking him, which was apt to be the result, the proceeding mounted at least one of our own troopers; on the other hand it gave a fresh horse to the enemy, and was equally lost to the owner—and this was the view the Virginians usually took of it. General Lee, being ahead of us, made a clean sweep as he went along, leaving scarce a gleaning of horseflesh for us. After a while we came upon the wagons and infantry again. It was not long before the ringing of a volley and the roar of a piece of artillery let us know that an attack had been made on our train again. We moved up to the firing at a gallop, and as we passed along there came sweeping through the woods, from the road running parallel with the one we were on, a body of infantry in line, moving at a double quick upon the same point, which was but a short distance ahead of us. They were what was left of the famous "Texas brigade," well remembered by some of us in 1861 on the Occoquon at Dumfries— first commanded by Wigfall, then a short time by Archer, then by Hood, then Gregg, who was killed October 26th, 1864, at the fight on the Darbytown road. At this time the brigade counted about one hundred and thirty muskets, commanded by Colonel Duke. We had been fighting with them all summer, from Deep Bottom to New Market heights, to the lines around Richmond, and they recognized the brigade as we rode along their front, and with a yell as fierce and keen as when their three regiments averaged a thousand strong, and nothing but victory had been around their flag, they shouted to us, "Forward, boys, forward, and tell them Texas is coming!"

When we got into the open field we found that General Lee's division of cavalry had engaged the enemy, driven him from his attack on our train, and taken the Federal General Gregg prisoner.

The enemy were occupying in force, apparently, the woods on the right of the field with infantry and artillery. We were holding the open field which had been the scene of the skirmish before we came up, and threw out skirmishers, and returned the fire of their sharpshooters—both sides using a piece or two of artillery at long range.

After this had gone on for a while, "ours," the Seventh, was ordered to charge in line on horseback, through a piece of old field, grown up in scattering pines, upon the battery that was working on us from the edge of the oak woods. The line was formed and we went at it very handsomely, our men keeping up their line and fire astonishingly, considering we were armed with "muzzle loaders" (the greatest possible of all drawbacks to the efficiency of cavalry).

We drew on ourselves at once a heavy fire of artillery and small arms, which told smartly on our line, knocking over men and horses, until the left flank of the regiment came upon a ravine, or deep wash, covering nearly half of its front. The horses could not cross. We moved by the right flank to clear the obstruction, and then found that the object of our demonstration had been answered. It had been made to cover the withdrawal of a body of our infantry that had been advanced on our right. It was sundown. We left a strong line of pickets, or rather a skirmish line, under command of Lieutenant Munerlyn, upon the ground we had occupied, and drew off into the open field, waiting for dark before going into camp, or rather lying on our arms. It had been a tiresome day, and, though neither then nor now an admirer of strong drink, I fell back upon and fully appreciated the contents of my canteen—the famous apple brandy of Amelia Springs.

This, although we did not know it then, was destined to be (save the last of all) the hardest night upon us. We moved into a piece of woods as soon as it was dark, and formed the regiment in squadrons, with orders to water horses, a squadron at a time—the rest holding position, the men in the saddle, until the return of the preceding squadron—and then picket their horses and make fires as near as possible on the same ground. But when the first squadron returned from the water, and the field officers had just unbuckled their sabres and stretched themselves on the ground to take the rest so much needed, and watch that most interesting process to a hungry man, the building up the little fire that was to do his modest cooking, when an orderly comes from General Gary to change camp—to buckle up and mount, and follow the orderly a half mile to the rear. We were, it seemed, too near the enemy's line, looking to the contemplated movement.

At the new location—a comfortable piece of piny woods old field—we finished what we had begun at the other point. At our mess, sleep seemed to be the great object in view. I went to sleep immediately, my head on my saddle ; woke in about a half hour's time to eat what there was, and instantly to sleep again ; but that was not to be. At about ten o'clock a quiet order mounted us, almost before, as the little boys say, we got the "sleep out of our eyes." We were in column on the road, and non-commissioned officers under the direction of the adjutant riding down it, each with a handkerchief full of cartridges, supplying the men with that very necessary "article of war." And then commenced that most weary night march, that will always be remembered by the tired men who rode it, that ended only (without a halt, except a marching one,) at Appomattox Courthouse.

The line of retreat had been changed, and by a forced night march on another road a push was being made for the mountains at Lynchburg. Had we gotten there (and Appomattox Court-house was within twenty miles of Lynchburg) with the men and material General Lee still had with him, Lee's last struggle among the mountains of his native State would have made a picture to swell the soldier's heart with pride to look upon. The end we know would have

been the same ; a few more noble hearts would have
bled in vain, and song and story would but have
found new themes to tell the old, old tale—how willing brave men are to die for what they believe to be
right. Through long lines of toiling wagons, artillery
trains and tired men, we pushed on as rapidly as we
could ; at a bad piece of road, at a creek or a muddy
hill, the column sometimes got cut in two by a portion getting through the wagons, the train then closing,
waiting upon a wagon mired down ahead.

At one of these halts for the brigade to close up
and for the regiments to report position, General Gary
had halted at a large fire made from the rails of some
good farmer's fence by troops ahead of us, and round
it we all gathered, for the night was cold. The
subject of conversation with the brigade staff when
we joined was, that Captain M., the inspector, not
being well, had, early in the night, halted at a farm
house and gone to bed, just to see how it would feel,
putting his horse in the farmer's stable ; and when
he roused himself to the necessities of his position,
and sought to ride with the rest, he found his horse
was gone. Some pressing party had gone that way.

I remembered, when I listened to the drowsy talk
about the captain's loss, that a couple of enterprising
young fellows had reported some horses at a farm
house and gotten permission to go after them. They
had not long returned with their prizes; they, the
horses, stood just on the edge of light thrown by the
fire against the darkness that rose like a wall behind

it, the hind-quarters of one, a large, leggy bay, with stockings on his hind legs, could be seen from where we sat; one of the orderlies, looking with sleepy eyes from the log on which he was sitting at the horses, expressed himself to the effect that he thought that "long-legged bay" looked about the hind-quarters a good deal like the captain's missing charger. And so it proved. While the captain "dallied at Capua," pressing the luxurious blanket of the Virginia farmer, his horse, in camp parlance, was "lifted" by our enterprising youth; and, much to their disgust, the captain reëntered into possession of his leggy war horse. They expressed themselves to the effect that they would as soon have stolen his horse as any body else's.

Again in the saddle, tramping through mud holes, splashing in ruts, we worked our way amid the long line of wagons, troops and artillery, until daylight came to our relief. About eight o'clock we came upon our own wagon train—the first, and, by the way, the only time we encountered it on our route—comfortably camped in a fine grove, good fires, and a glorious smell of cooking permeating the early morning air. The headquarter wagons of our regiment were parked near a fine fire, and our servants (never expecting to see us again, I suppose,) were cooking on a large scale from our private stores for a half dozen notorious wagon-rats of the genteeler sort.

Of course, as we rode up our boys declared they expected us and were getting breakfast ready, which statement was sustained by "messieurs," the wagon-rats; but the longing look they cast at a big pot of rice steaming by the fire as they drew off, indicated a deeper interest than I think it possible for them to have gotten up on any one's account but their own. We had a most comfortable breakfast and a rest of an hour only, the time being taken up in dozing and eating.

Bad as the night had been the day was a beautiful one. The sun was shining bright; our breakfast and rest had so refreshed us, short as that rest was, that we resumed our march and the work before us, cheerful and ready to meet it, whatever it might be, and what that "might be" was no man troubled himself to know.

Not long after resuming our march we posted pickets at some cross roads, under the immediate direction of General R. E. Lee himself. We moved steadily on to-day without molestation of any kind, the wagons moving in double lines, the road being wide enough to admit it. About twelve o'clock or a little later we had halted to water our horses at a stream that crossed the road. It takes a good deal of time for a large body of cavalry to water their horses, particularly if the stream is small, and the men have to be watched closely to prevent their fouling the water.

I had dismounted and was leaning across my horse, when I saw, as I thought, Captain Allen, of the Twenty-fourth Virginia, of our brigade, having watered his horse where the stream crossed the road. The captain was a fine specimen of a Virginia soldier and gentleman, some sixty years of age, of fine presence, who was always said to resemble General Lee, wearing his grey beard trimmed after the fashion of that of our great leader, and in the saddle having about the same height, though dismounted, the captain, I should say, was the taller. However, I watched the old captain, as I thought, riding up the hill toward me, on a very fine grey horse, and was thinking what a type of the veteran soldier he looked, as indeed I had often thought before, until he got within a few feet of me, when I changed my intended rather familiar, but still most respectful salute, meant for the captain, for the reverence with which the soldier salutes the standard of his legion—which represents to him all that he has left to love and honor—as I discovered that it was General R. E. Lee himself, riding alone—not even an orderly in attendance. He returned our salute, his eye taking it all in, with a calm smile, that assured us our confidence was not misplaced. He bore the pressure of the responsibility that was upon him as only a great and good man could—as one who felt that, happen what may, selfishness—consideration of what might happen to himself—had nothing to do with it.

So I felt satisfied that there was a likeness between Captain Allen, of the Twenty-fourth Virginia, and General R. E. Lee of the Southern Confederacy.

A little after this we got orders to move on, as

quickly as we could, in advance to Appomattox Court-house. "Appomattox Court-house" is a small county town about a mile from the Lynchburg railroad. At the foot of the hill on which the courthouse and the three or four houses that constitute the village stand, run the headwaters of the Appomattox river, a small stream, not knee deep to a horse.

As soon as we cleared the wagon train we got over ground much faster, and rode into and through the town just as the sun was setting. We stopped at a piece of woods on the outskirts of the village, and halted in the road while the quartermasters were selecting the ground, and the regiments were closing up. Our foragers, that had been detailed before we got into town, were riding in with the hay they had collected on the pommels of their saddles, and all was as quiet as a scene in "Arcady," when the stillness was broken by the scream of a shell, the report of a gun, and then the burst-up of the missile as it finished its mission and reported progress—and then another, and another, until as pretty battery practice was developed down yonder by the depot—Clover Hill I think it is called—as you would wish to hear.

Without knowing positively anything about it, those whom I had conversed with relative to our pushing on to the Court house were under the impression that a large body of our infantry were ahead of us—General Dick Anderson's corps. He was there, as it turned out, but his corps had been expended a day or two before; it had been completely fought out, for we had no better officer than Lt. General Richard Anderson, an old West Pointer—cavalry at that—and a South Carolinian to boot.

It was, however, "hammer and tongs" down there at all events—shell, grape and canister at short range. Custar's division of Sheridan's cavalry had taken the chord of the arc, and reached the depot just about the time we got to the village. A knowledge of his movements had caused our being sent forward, his object being to strike the artillery train, which was in advance of us—sixty pieces, under General Walker. Three batteries were left at the depot to hold it, while the rest retreated along the Lynchburg pike. The three batteries were six guns under command of Major James C. Coit—consisting of two guns Pegram's battery, Va., Lieut. Scott; two guns Wright's battery, Va., Lieut. Atkisson; two guns Martin's battery, Va., Capt. Martin; with sixteen men, Kelly's battery, S. C., Lieut. Race, who assisted in working Wright's guns.

While we were closing up our scattered ranks, and getting the brigade ready for action as rapidly as coolness, skill and courage could do it, a department officer (I think he was) came galloping up to us from the scene of action, apparently under orders from himself to get out of the way; but the natural insolence of his class broke out in spite of the scare that was on him, and he commenced giving orders at once. I happened to be the person addressed—" Get on at once; the enemy are down yonder Why don't you go at once? Are all you men going to stand here and let the enemy "—and so on. The colonel had ridden down the column to see that all was straight, while the "Legion" and the Twenty-fourth Virginia were closing up, so that when we did move it would be as a compact body—when the order came ringing along—"Forward, forward, men! gallop!"—and our indignant friend was lost in the rush of the column while yet haranguing us for being so slow.

The roar of the batteries was incessant. They were evidently holding the dismounted cavalry in check. As rapidly as we could get over ground we moved towards them, and formed the brigade in the field to the left of the position held by the batteries, in what might be called a column of regiments. As we formed the regiment from a column of fours into line, they came down from a gallop to a trot at the order, "Front into line," as steadily as if on parade; then followed, "Right dress, front"—and all were ready for the next move.

Our batteries from the right were shelling the woods opposite to us. In front, under cover, some of the cavalry skirmishers were using their Spencers upon us at long range, and a squadron of ours, the Fifth, was detailed to move up and take a position opposite and return their fire.

By this time the grey of twilight was lighted up by the rising moon, and there seemed to be a lull in the attack. General Gary and Colonel Haskell had ridden over our front and communicated with the commanding officer of the batteries; the consequence of which was, the brigade was dismounted and double-quicked through a small piece of wood to the batteries. Before our men could get to the guns the enemy charged and got among them, but were driven back by the fire and our rush, but taking with them some of our men as prisoners—among them Captain Hankins, of the Virginia battery, who got away and came running up to me as I rode to my place. Our men fell in between the guns, and then began one of the closest artillery fights, for the numbers engaged and the time it lasted, that occurred during the war. The guns were fought literally up to the muzzles. It was dark by this time, and at every discharge the cannon was ablaze from touch-hole to mouth, and there must have been six or eight pieces at work, and the small arms of some three or four hundred men packed in among the guns in a very confined space. It seemed like the very jaws of the lower regions. They made three distinct charges, preluding always with the bugle, on the right, left and centre, confusing the point of attack; then, with a cheer and up they came. It was too dark to see anything under the shadow of the trees but the long dark line. They would get within thirty or forty yards of the guns and then roll back, under the deadly fire that was poured upon them from the artillery and small arms. Amid the flashing, and the roaring, and the shouting, rose the wild yell of a railroad whistle, as a train rushed up almost among us (the enemy had possession of the road), as we were fighting around the depot, sounding on the night air as if the devil himself. had just come up and was about to join in what was going on.

Then came a lull; our friends in front seemed to have had the wire edge taken off.

Our horses had been sent back to the turnpike road; General Gary taking advantage of the present quiet sent Colonel Haskell to get them together—rather a difficult task, as it afterwards proved.

General Gary's great object was to draw off the guns, if possible, now night had set in, from the depot, and get them back with the rest of the train in the line of retreat. So the order was given to limber them up, which was done, and the guns moved off at once, it being but a few hundred yards to the main road.

Our brigade in line faced to the rear, the guns behind them, and covered the movement. The silence of the guns soon told our friends over yonder what was going on, and they were not long in following after; our men, facing to the rear, delivered their fire steadily, moving in retreat, facing and firing every few steps, effectually keeping off a rush; they pressed us, but cautiously—the darkness concealed our numbers.

We were going through an open old field, and came now to a road through a narrow piece of woods. where we broke from line into column, and double-quicked through the woods so as to get to the road beyond. Before we got to the turnpike we heard the bugles of the enemy down it, and as the head of our column came into the road their cavalry charged the train some two or three hundred yards below us. Sixty pieces of cannon, at the point where we came into the road, the drivers were attempting to turn back toward the Court House, had got entangled with one another and presented a scene of utter confusion.

As our regiment got into the road some thirty or forty men were thrown out from the last squadron and faced to the rear on the right and left, opening a fire directly upon those of the dismounted men who were pressing us from that quarter. I had but little fear of the enemy's cavalry riding into us on the road, so blocked up as it was with the routed artillery train, and there were woods on both sides just here.

In passing from the old field, where the guns had been at work, into the woods that separated it from the turnpike, two men were walking just in front of me, following their gun, which was on before. I heard one say, "*Tout perdu.*" I asked at once, "What battery do you belong to?" "Donaldsonville." It was the creole company; and they might well have added the other words of the great Francis, after the battle of Pavia, "*Tout perdu fors l'honneur,*" all lost but honor; for well had they done their work from 'sixty-one, when they came to Virginia, until now, when all was lost, "*Tout perdu*"—it was the motto of the occasion.

The stag was in the toils, but the end was not yet.

We could hear the rush, the shouts and pistol shots, where the enemy mounted and in force had attacked the train; the artillerymen having no arms could make no fight, as they could not use their pieces. We could do nothing (being closely pressed by a superior force of their dismounted men) but fall back upon the town toward our main body, making the best front we could, leaving the road and marching under cover of the timber on the side, being on foot giving us a better position to resist any attack that might be made upon us by the cavalry.

The fifth squadron of the Seventh, that had been thrown out as skirmishers when we first came on the ground, had kept their position covering our left flank when the fight at the batteries was going on. And when we commenced falling back after the guns, the adjutant, Lieutenant Capers, was sent to bring them to the road, so as to join the regiment. They had also been dismounted, and their horses sent with the rest. He found them, led them to the road, and, on getting on it at a point nearer to the town than where we struck it, hearing the bugles and the rush of the cavalry on the train, he at once posted the companies, with their captains, Doby and Dubose, in the woods immediately on the road-side, and with the parting salutation, "Take care of yourselves, boys," (he had been a private in one of the companies, and both were from his native district), dashed back to his place in the regiment and disappeared round a turn in the road. They had scarcely lost sight of him when a heavy volley rang out, and his horse came round the bend at full speed without his rider, jumping over in his fright a broken caisson that lay across the road —the horse, a very fine roan, the one he was riding when, at "Amelia Spring," he, Capers, was the only one of the five in advance who escaped, to meet his fate that night, pierced by a dozen balls; the whole fire of the column was concentrated upon him, for we found his body next day. Some kind hand had given him a soldier's grave; some one, most likely of those who fought us, who could not but respect and admire the gallant young fellow lying in his blood, and with the feeling developed by a soldier's life, "So be it to me and mine in my sorrow as I may be to thee this day." All the respect was shown that circumstances admitted of.

One of our captains, who was wounded at the "guns" severely, fell into the enemy's hands when we moved them—as everybody was too busy to look after the wounded, and ambulance men and stretchers were this time neither in the front or rear. He was taken up by his new friends quite tenderly, as he thought, and put into an ambulance; but in the course of the evening's entertainment the Yankee wounded came dropping in, and our friend, Captain Walker, was disposed of rather unceremoniously on the roadside, for others they valued at a higher rate than even a Confederate captain.

Immediately after the adjutant's horse came Custar's cavalry. Seeing all clear before them, they

THE NEW YORK
PUBLIC LIBRARY.

ASTOR, LENOX AND
TILDEN FOU'

came on without a check until, when nearly opposite where our men of the Fifth squadron were lying in the woods, they caught the fire of the entire squadron, which emptied a good many saddles, and was the last shot probably fired that night.

The Federal cavalry kept on toward the town, and the squadron, under cover, drew deeper into the woods, and moved round the town and went into camp, but did not join the main body until next morning. The enemy kept on until they got into, or nearly into the town, but again fell back, establishing their line somewhere between the town and the depot. Our outside picket was in the town.

We went into camp about one o'clock in the morning, on the Richmond side of the town, in the woods— General Gary riding to General Gordon's headquarters to report before lying down.

April 9th.—The sun rose clear on this the last day, practically, of the Southern Confederacy. It was cool and fresh in the early morning so near the mountains, though the spring must have been a forward one, as the oak trees were covered with their long yellow tassels.

We gathered the brigade on the green on the Richmond side of the village, most of the men on foot, the horses not having come in. About eight o'clock a large portion of our regiment had their horses— they having been completely cut off the night before by the charge of Custar's cavalry on the turnpike, and were carried, to save them, into a country cross-road.

Then the "Hampton Legion" got theirs. My impression is that the Twenty-fourth Virginia lost the most or a good many of their horses. The men built fires, and all seemed to have something to eat, and to be amusing themselves eating it. The woods on the southern and eastern side swarmed with the enemy and their cavalry—a portion of it was between us and the "James River," which was about twelve miles distant. General Fitz Lee's division of cavalry lay over in that direction somewhere; General Longstreet with General Gordon was in and on the outer edge of the town, on the Lynchburg side, and so we waited for the performance to commence.

Looking at and listening to the men you would not have thought there was anything special in the situation. They turned all the responsibility over to the officers, who in turn did the same to those above them—the captain to the colonel, the colonel to the brigadier, and so on.

Colonel Haskell had not yet returned—having sent in all the horses he had gotten, and was still after the balance. About nine or ten o'clock, artillery firing began in front of General Longstreet, and the blue jackets showed in heavy masses on the edge of the woods. General Gary riding up, put everything that had a horse in the saddle, and moved us down the hill, just on the edge of the little creek that is here the "Appomattox," to wait under cover until wanted. Two of our young men, who had some flour and a piece of bacon in their haversacks, had improvised a cooking utensil out of a bursted canteen, and fried some cakes. They offered me a share in their meal, of which I partook with great relish. I then lay down, with my head, like the luxurious Highlander, upon a smooth stone, and, holding my horse's bridle in my hand, was soon in the deep sleep of a tired man. But not for long, for down came the general in his most emphatic manner—and those who know Gary know a man whose emphasis can be wonderfully strong when so minded. "Mount, men, mount!" I jumped up at the sharp, ringing summons with the sleep still in my eyes, and found myself manœuvring my horse with his rear in front. We soon had everything in its right place, and rode out from the bottom into the open field, about two hundred and fifty strong, to see the last of it.

Firing was going on, artillery and small arms, beyond the town, and there was General R. E. Lee himself, with Longstreet, Gordon, and the rest of his paladins.

When we rode into the open field we could see the enemy crowding along the edge of the woods—cavalry apparently extending their line around us. We kept on advancing towards them to get a nearer view of things, and were midway on the Richmond side between the town and a large white house with a handsome grove around it. In the yard could be seen a body of cavalry, in number about our own; we saw no other troops near. Two or three hundred yards to the right of the house an officer, apparently of rank, with a few men—his staff, probably—riding well forward, halted, looking toward the town with his glass. Just as he rode out General Gary had given the order to charge the party in the yard. Some one remarked that it looked like a flag of truce. "Charge!" swore Gary in his roughest tones, and on we went. The party in the yard were taken by surprise; they had not expected us to charge them, as they were aware that a parley was going on (of which, of course, we knew nothing), and that there was a suspension of hostilities.

We drove them through the yard, taking one or two prisoners—one little fellow, who took it very good-humoredly; he had his head tied up, having got it broken somewhere on the road, and was riding a mule. We followed up their retreat through the yard, down a road, through the open woods beyond, and were having it, as we thought, all our own way—when, stretched along behind the brown oaks, and moving with a close and steady tramp, was a long line of cavalry, some thousands strong—Custar's division—our friends of last night. This altered the complexion of things entirely; the order was instantly given to move by the left flank—which, without throwing our back to them, changed the forward into a retrograde movement.

The enemy kept his line unbroken, pressing slowly forward, firing no volley, but dropping shots from a line of scattered skirmishers in front was all we got. They, of course, knew the condition of things, and seemed to think we did not. We fell back toward a battery of ours that was behind us, supported, I think, by a brigade of North Carolina infantry. We moved slowly, and the enemy's skirmishers got close enough for a dash to be made by our acting regimental adjutant—in place of Lieutenant Capers, killed the night before—Lieutenant Haile, who took a prisoner, but just as it was done one of our couriers —Tribble, Seventh regiment—mounted on a fine black horse, bareheaded, dashed between the two lines with a handkerchief tied upon a switch, sent by General Gordon, announcing the "suspension of hostilities."

By this time the enterprising adjutant had in turn been made prisoner. As soon as the orders were understood everything came to a stand-still, and for a while I thought we were going to have, then and there, a little inside fight on purely personal grounds.

An officer—a captain—I presume the captain in command of the party in the yard that we had attacked and driven back upon the main body—had, I rather expect, been laughed at by his own people for his prompt and sudden return from the expedition he had set out on.

He rode up at once to General Gary, and with a good deal of heat (he had his drawn sabre in his hand) wanted to know what he, Gary, meant by keeping up the fight after there had been a surrender. "Surrender!" said Gary, "I have heard of no surrender. We are South Carolinians, and don't surrender. [Ah! General, but we did, though.] Besides, sir, I take commands from no officers but my own, and I do not recognize you or any of your cloth as such."

The rejoinder was about to be a harsh one, sabres were out and trouble was very near, when an officer of General Custar's staff—I should like to have gotten his name—his manner was in striking contrast to that of the bellicose captain, who seemed rather to belong to the snorting persuasion—he, with the language and manner of a thorough gentleman, said, "I assure you, General, and I appreciate your feelings in the matter, that there has been a suspension of hostilities, pending negotiations, and General Lee and General Grant are in conference on the matter at this time."

His manner had its effect on General Gary, who at once sheathed his sabre, saying, "Do not suppose, sir, I have any doubt of the truth of your statement, but you must allow that, under such circumstances, I can only receive orders from my own officers; but I am perfectly willing to accept your statement and wait for those orders." (Situated as we were, certainly a wise conclusion.) Almost on the instant Colonel Blackford, of the engineers, rode up, sent by General Gordon, with a Federal officer, carrying orders to that effect.

We drew back to the artillery and infantry that were just behind us, and formed our battered fragments into regiments.

Desperate as we knew our condition to be since last

night's affair, still the idea of a complete surrender, which we began now to see was inevitable, came as an awful shock. Men came to their officers with tears streaming from their eyes, and asked what it all meant, and would, at that moment, I know, have rather died the night before than see the sun rise on such a day as this.

And so the day wore on, and the sun went down, and with it the hopes of a people who, with prayers, and tears, and blood, had striven to uphold that falling flag.

It was all too true, and our worst fears were fully justified by the result. The suspension of hostilities was but a prelude to surrender, which was, when it came to a show of hands, inevitable.

General Lee's army had been literally pounded to pieces after the battle of "Five Forks," around Petersburg, which made the evacuation of Richmond and the retreat a necessity. When General Longstreet's corps from the north bank joined it, the "army of Northern Virginia," wasted and reduced to skeleton battalions, was still an army of veteran material, powerful yet for attack or defence, all the more dangerous from its desperate condition. And General Grant so recognized and dealt with it, attacking it, as before stated, in detail; letting it wear itself out by straggling and the disorganizing effect of a retreat, breaking down of men and material. The infantry were almost starved.

It was not until the fourth day from Richmond, at

the high bridge on the "Appomattox," the battle of Sailor's Creek was fought, in which, with overwhelming masses of cavalry, artillery and infantry, our starved and tired men were ridden down, and General Grant destroyed, in military parlance, the divisions of Kershaw, Ewell, Anderson and Custis Lee.

The fighting next day was of the same desultory character as before, and the day after there was no blow struck until we encountered with the artillery Custar's cavalry, at the depot of Appomattox Courthouse, as has been described—all their energies being directed toward establishing their "cordon" around that point.

The terms of the surrender, and all about it, are too well known to go over in detail here—prisoners of war on parole, officers to retain side arms, and all private property to be respected, that was favorable to our cavalry, as in the Confederate service the men all owned their horses, though different in the United States army, the horses belonging to Government.

General Gary, true to the doctrine he had laid down in his discussion with the irate captain, that "South Carolinians did not surrender," turned his horse's head, and, with Captain Doby and one or two others, managed to get that night through the "cordon" drawn around us, and succeeded in reaching Charlotte, North Carolina, which became, for a time, the headquarters of the "Southern Confederacy"—the President and his Cabinet having established themselves there.

Colonel Haskell, who had been separated from us the night before, while gathering up the horses of the brigade, by the charge of cavalry on the turnpike, and had joined and been acting with General Walker and his artillery, came in about two o'clock. All the Confederate cavalry at Appomattox, some two thousand or twenty-five hundred, were under his command as ranking officer.

The brigade crossed the road and bivouacked in the open field near the creek, within a few hundred yards of the town. Our infantry, and what was left of the artillery, was scattered along the road for two or three miles toward Richmond—the enemy swarming in every direction around us, and occupying the town as headquarters.

The articles of capitulation were signed next morning under the famous "apple tree," I suppose; what we saw of it was this: General Lee was seen, dressed in full Confederate uniform, with his sword on, riding his fine grey charger, and accompanied by General Gordon, coming from the village, and riding immediately in front of where we were lying. He had not been particularly noticed as he had gone toward the town, for, though with the regiment, I have no recollection of his doing so. As soon as he was seen it acted like an electric flash upon our men; they sprang to their feet, and, running to the roadside, commenced a wild cheering that roused our troops. As far as we could see they came running down the hill sides, and joining in, along the ground, and through the woods, and up into the sky, there went a tribute that has seldom been paid to mortal man. " Faithful, though all was lost!"

The Federal army officers and men bore themselves toward us as brave men should. I do not recollect, within my personal observation, a single act that could be called discourteous—nor did I hear of one. On the other hand, much kindness and consideration were exhibited when circumstances made it warrantable—such as previous acquaintance, as was common among the officers of the old army, or a return of kindness when parties had been prisoners in our hands, as was the case with a portion of the Seventh regiment when it was the cavalry battalion of the Holcomb Legion, under Colonel Shingler, and the Fifth Pennsylvania cavalry.

Regular rations were issued to men and horses. An apology was offered, on one occasion, by the Federal Quartermaster, for not serving out horse feed, as General F. Lee's division of cavalry, who were, as I mentioned before, outside, up in the James River direction, had cut off a wagon train that held their provender, so we had to send out a forage detail in the neighborhood, with a pass from General Sheridan, to get through the Federal troops that filled the woods for miles around, for their name was legion. We stacked eight thousand stands of arms, all told; artillery, cavalry, infantry stragglers, wagon-rats, and all the rest, from twelve to fifteen thousand men. The United States troops, by their own estimate, were 150,000 men, with a railroad connecting their rear with Washington, New York, Germany, France, Belgium, Africa, "all the world and the rest of mankind," as General Taylor comprehensively remarked, for their recruiting stations were all over the world, and the crusade against the South, and its peculiar manners and civilization, under the pressure of the "almighty American dollar," was as absolute and varied in its nationality as was that of "Peter the Hermit," under the pressure of religious zeal, upon Jerusalem.

Success had made them good natured. Those we came in contact with were soldiers—fighting men—and, as is always the case, such appreciate their position and are too proud to bear themselves in any other way. They, in the good nature of success, were more willing to give than our men, in the soreness of defeat, to receive.

The effect of such conduct upon our men was of the best kind; the unexpected consideration shown by the officers and men of the United States army towards us; the heartiness with which a Yankee soldier would come up to a Confederate officer and say, "We have been fighting one another for four years; give me a Confederate five dollar bill to remember you by," had nothing in it offensive.

They were proud of their success, and we were not ashamed of our defeat; and not a man of that grand army of one hundred and fifty thousand men but could, and I believe would, testify, that, n purely personal grounds, the few worn-out half-starved men that gathered around General Lee and his falling flag held the prouder position of the two. Had the politicians left things alone, such feelings would have resulted in a very different condition of things.

Those of us who took serious consideration of the state of affairs, felt that with our defeat we had as absolutely lost our country—the one we held under the Constitution—as though we had been conquered and made a colony of by France or Russia. The right of the strongest—the law of the sword—was as absolute at "Appomattox" that day as when Brennus, the Gaul, threw it in the scale at the ransom of Rome.

So far, it was all according to the order of things, and we stood on the bare hills men without a country. General Grant offered us, it was said, rations and transportation—each man to his native State, now a conquered province, or to Halifax, Nova Scotia. Many would not have hesitated to accept the offer for Halifax and rations; but, in distant Southern homes were old men, helpless women and children, whose cry for help it was not hard to hear. So, in good faith, accepting our fate, we took allegiance to this, our new country, which is now called the "United States," as we would have done to France or Russia.

With all that was around us—the destruction of the "Army of Northern Virginia," and certain defeat of the Confederacy as the result—no one dreamed of what has followed. The fanaticism that has influenced the policy of the Government, to treat subject States, whose citizens had been permitted to take an oath of allegiance, accepted them as such, and promised to give them the benefit of laws protecting person, property and religion, as the dominant party in the United States has done—exceeds belief.

To place the government of the States absolutely in the hands of its former slaves, and call their "acts" "laws;" to denounce the slightest effort to assert the white vote, even under the laws, treason; and, finally, force the unwilling United States soldier to use his bayonet to sustain the grossest outrages of law and decency against men of his own color and race! This has gone on until, lost in wonder as to what is to come next, the southern white man watches events, as a tide that is gradually rising and spreading, and from which he sees no avenue of escape, and must, unless an intervention almost miraculous takes place, soon sweep him away.